WELCOME TO MY COUNTRY

Welcome to HAITI

Gareth Stevens Publishing

A WORLD ALMANAC EDUCATION GROUP COMPANY

Written by
KATHARINE BROWN/MICHELE WAGNER

Edited by
MELVIN NEO

Edited in USA by
DOROTHY L. GIBBS

Designed by
GEOSLYN LIM

Picture research by
SUSAN JANE MANUEL

First published in North America in 2003 by
Gareth Stevens Publishing
A World Almanac Education Group Company
330 West Olive Street, Suite 100
Milwaukee, Wisconsin 53212 USA

Please visit our web site at:
www.garethstevens.com
For a free color catalog describing
Gareth Stevens Publishing's list of high-quality
books and multimedia programs,
call 1-800-542-2595 (USA) or
1-800-387-3178 (Canada).
Gareth Stevens Publishing's fax: (414) 332-3567.

© **TIMES MEDIA PRIVATE LIMITED 2003**
Originated and designed by Times Editions
An imprint of Times Media Private Limited
A member of the Times Publishing Group
Times Centre, 1 New Industrial Road
Singapore 536196
http://www.timesone.com.sg/te

Library of Congress Cataloging-in-Publication Data
Brown, Katharine Elizabeth, 1972–
Welcome to Haiti / Katharine Brown and Michele Wagner.
p. cm. — (Welcome to my country)
Summary: An overview of the geography, history,
government, economy, people, and culture of Haiti.
Includes bibliographical references and index.
ISBN 0-8368-2551-9 (lib. bdg.)
1. Haiti—Juvenile literature. [1. Haiti.]
I. Wagner, Michele, 1975– . II. Title. III. Series.
F1915.2.B76   2003
972.92—dc21   2003041785

Printed in Singapore

1 2 3 4 5 6 7 8 9 07 06 05 04 03

Contents

Words that appear in the glossary are printed in **boldface** type the first
time they occur in the text.

Welcome to Haiti!

As part of Hispaniola Island, in the Caribbean Sea, Haiti was ruled first by the Spanish, then by the French, before gaining independence in 1804. After many years of **corrupt** leadership, the Haitian **republic** is now rebuilding a **democratic** government. Let's learn more about Haiti and its people.

Opposite:
This Haitian driver's colorful car is one of many brightly painted vehicles in the busy capital city of Port-au-Prince.

Below:
Huge baskets of bread are a common sight at Haiti's many outdoor markets.

The Flag of Haiti

Haiti's national flag has two horizontal bands. One is blue, and one is red. A white rectangle in the center of the flag contains the country's **coat of arms**. The French words beneath the coat of arms mean "union makes strength."

The Land

With an area of 10,641 square miles (27,560 square kilometers), Haiti covers about one-third of Hispaniola, on the western side of the island. Its eastern neighbor, the Dominican Republic, covers the remaining two-thirds of Hispaniola. The Atlantic Ocean is off Haiti's northern coast. The Caribbean Sea is to the west and the south. Haiti has two **peninsulas** and includes four other islands.

Below: Haiti has many magnificent coves, bays, and beaches along its 1,100 miles (1,770 kilometers) of coastline.

Mountain ranges divide Haiti into three regions — northern, central, and southern — and mountains cover more than two-thirds of the land. Pic la Selle, in southeastern Haiti, is, at 8,793 feet (2,680 meters), the country's highest peak. Many rivers flow down Haiti's mountains. The Artibonite, the largest and the only **navigable** river, flows east to west toward the Caribbean Sea.

Above: The rich green fields in Haiti's northern region are good for farming. Only about 20 percent of the country's land is suitable for growing crops.

Climate

Haiti's climate is mainly tropical, but rainfall and temperatures are different in each of the country's three regions. The south has two rainy seasons. The northern and central regions have only one, and they are at different times of the year. Overall, the worst storms hit between June and October. In lowland areas, the annual average temperature is 80° Fahrenheit (27° Celsius). In the mountains, temperatures are cooler but rarely average below 60° F (16° C).

Below: Some farmers still ride donkeys home from a day's work in the fields of southeastern Haiti. The climate in this area is hot and dry all year because high mountains block the winds that blow in from the coast.

Left: The manatee is an **endangered** sea animal that makes its home in some of Haiti's lakes and swamps.

Plants and Animals

Clearing trees to create farmland has destroyed most of Haiti's forests. Pine forests, however, have survived high in the mountains, **mangroves** can still be found in Haiti's swamps, and palm trees are scattered all over the country. Plants found in the desertlike lowlands are mainly cactus or **scrub**.

Hunting has destroyed many of Haiti's native animals. Small animals, such as butterflies, frogs, and bats, still live in the mountains, and desert areas still have lizards and snakes.

Above: The endangered peregrine falcon spends its winters in Haiti. More than eighty species of birds still live in the country's mountain areas.

9

History

The Taino were the first settlers on Hispaniola Island. They called the land Ayiti. When Spanish explorers led by Christopher Columbus arrived on the island in 1492, they traded with the Taino for gold. Thinking that Ayiti had rich mineral resources, Spain **colonized** the island. By 1550, the Spanish had destroyed the Taino **civilization**.

Left:
This drawing by a sixteenth-century European artist shows a Taino man and woman on the island of Ayiti. The Taino had lived on Ayiti for hundreds of years before the Spanish arrived.

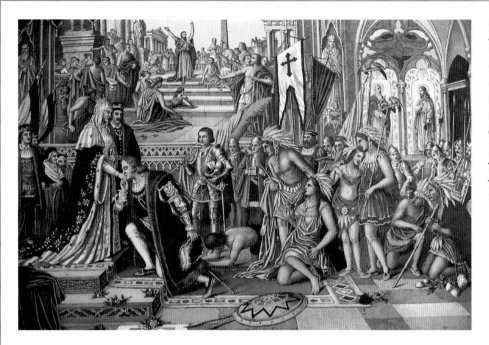

Left:
When Columbus returned to Spain, he brought Taino people with him. In this nineteenth-century painting, he is presenting the Taino people to the Spanish king and queen.

In 1697, Spain gave control of the western part of Hispaniola to France. By the mid-1700s, Ayiti, which had been renamed Saint-Domingue, was the richest colony in the Americas.

Most of the people living on Saint-Domingue were black slaves that the French brought from Africa to work on plantations. The slaves were treated cruelly and did not have rights of any kind. **Mulattoes** could own land, but only white people could hold political power. In 1791, black slaves revolted against the white government.

An Independent Nation

After more than ten years of fighting, the slaves defeated the French. Haiti became independent on January 1, 1804. Its first emperor, Jean-Jacques Dessalines (c.1758–1806), ruled for only two years. He was **assassinated** in 1806. By 1915, with over twenty-two changes in leadership, Haiti had become very **unstable**. After president Guillaume Sam **executed** 167 political prisoners, the United States stepped in and governed Haiti for nineteen years.

Above: Before he declared himself emperor of Haiti, Jean-Jacques Dessalines (*left*) was a rebel fighter who helped the slaves defeat the French. In 1811, Henri Christophe (c.1767–1820) (*right*) declared himself king of Haiti. He ruled northern Haiti until he died.

The Duvalier Era

By 1934, the United States had left Haiti, and the nation had no central government, so the Haitian military took control. In 1957, the military helped Dr. François Duvalier become president. Known as "Papa Doc," Duvalier ruled as a **dictator** until his death in 1971. His son, Jean-Claude, who was called "Baby Doc," became Haiti's next president.

Below: Papa Doc's police force was called the *Tonton Macoutes* (tohn-tohn mah-KOOT). These soldiers kept Papa Doc in power by terrorizing the Haitian people. The Tonton Macoutes killed about 30,000 Haitians during Papa Doc's rule.

Becoming a Democracy

When protests broke out against him, Baby Doc Duvalier fled to France, and from 1986 to 1990, Haiti was ruled by temporary governments. Jean-Bertrand Aristide (1953–) was elected president in 1990 but, within seven months, was overthrown by the military. Aristide returned to power in 1994. From 1996 to 2000, René Préval (1943–) was Haiti's president. In 2000, Aristide was reelected and is now trying to establish a stronger democracy in Haiti.

Left: Jean-Claude Duvalier (1951–) became Haiti's president in 1971. Violent protests against "Baby Doc's" corrupt leadership forced him to leave the country in 1986.

François Macandal (?–1758)

In 1751, African François Macandal led runaway slaves in a rebellion against French plantation owners that lasted six years. The French captured and killed Macandal in 1758.

Simone Ovide Duvalier (1913–1997)

Simone Ovide Duvalier

Known as "Mama Doc," Simone Ovide was married to Haitian president François "Papa Doc" Duvalier. When their son Jean-Claude was president, Simone ruled the country because "Baby Doc" had no interest in politics.

René Garcia Préval (1943–)

René Garcia Préval

Active in the movement against Jean-Claude Duvalier, René Garcia Préval became Haiti's prime minister in 1991 and was the country's elected president from 1996 to 2000.

Government and the Economy

Haiti is an independent republic led by a president and a prime minister. The president is elected by the people and serves a five-year term. The prime minister is appointed by the president. Both leaders are responsible for the nation's defense and for appointing other government ministers.

Below: Haiti's president lives in the Palais National, or National Palace. It is located in the capital city of Port-au-Prince.

Left: This group of Haitian soldiers is marching in front of government buildings in Port-au-Prince. The Palais National is in the background.

Haiti's Parliament supervises the activities of the president and the prime minister and approves all government appointments, as well as all new laws. It is made up of a Chamber of Deputies and a Senate. Both the Chamber and the Senate have elected members.

The country's legal system includes a variety of courts with different levels of authority. The Cour de Cessation, or Supreme Court, is the highest court in the nation.

A Struggling Economy

Largely because of Haiti's corrupt government leaders, its economy has been struggling for many years. The nation depends heavily on help from other countries, and about 80 percent of its people live in extreme **poverty**.

Most of Haiti's poorest people are farmers. In spite of problems such as poor farming methods, **deforestation**, and **erosion**, about two-thirds of the workforce is employed in agriculture.

Below: Sugarcane is one of the most important crops in Haiti, and many Haitians work in the sugarcane fields. Juice that comes from the cane they gather is used to manufacture sugar and molasses.

Industries and Transportation

About 25 percent of Haiti's workforce have manufacturing jobs in industries such as clothing, chemicals, steel, and food products. Most of the remaining workforce is employed in **commerce**, tourism, or other service industries.

Poor transportation has added to Haiti's economic struggle. The country has only one international airport, no working railroads, and, except for the highways, most of the roads are just dirt or gravel.

Above:
For transporting products into and out of the country, Haiti has a number of seaports. This port is in the city of Cap-Haïtien. Other port cities include Port-au-Prince, Gonaïves, Jacmel, and Saint-Marc.

People and Lifestyle

Ninety-five percent of Haitian people are blacks of African descent. The rest are whites or mulattoes. Although the number of whites and mulattoes is small, they make up most of Haiti's upper class. Upper-class Haitians are educated, cultured, and wealthy, and their lifestyles include many French traditions. The wealthiest Haitians live in private communities.

Below:
Haitian women, both mulatto (*left*) and African (*right*), are strong and lead active lives. Even women in poor rural areas are involved in various types of trade and commerce.

Left: Besides unhealthy living conditions and little, if any, clean water, Haiti has a very poor health care system. Three out of every twenty Haitian children die before age five.

Most of Haiti's poor population, or lower classes, live in rural areas, where they try to farm land that is not suitable for growing crops. Few rural Haitians have access to clean water, and many are too far away from schools to send their children. Living conditions for lower-class Haitians in the cities are even worse than for the rural poor.

A small number of Arabs make up Haiti's only **ethnic minority**. Most Haitian-Arabs have lighter skin, speak French, and have upper-class lifestyles.

Family Life

Traditionally, Haitian families were very large, especially in rural areas. These large families, called extended families, included grandparents, uncles, aunts, and cousins. All members of an extended family could depend on each other for help and support. Although, today, Haitians still have strong family ties, most of them do not have enough money or space for an extended family. Parents work very hard to provide for their children. In return, grown children take care of their aging parents.

Left: To Haitian parents, children are gifts from God. Even the poorest parents try to make sure their children go to school. They know that getting an education is the only way the children will have better lives.

The Roles of Men and Women

Haitian men and women usually share responsibilities. Although women raise the children and do most of the work around the house, men do the heavy chores, such as gathering firewood. In rural areas, women help their husbands in the fields, and many Haitian women have jobs outside the home. Except for money made from farming, women do not have to share what they earn with their husbands.

Above: Women from Haiti's farms often travel to local markets to sell the crops and animals they raise, but they do not have to give any of the money from the sales to their husbands.

Education

All children in Haiti are required to go to school, but problems, such as living too far from a school, keep many of them from attending regularly. In 1978, the Haitian government made changes in the country's education system that help it better meet the needs of children from poor families. Still, many parents cannot afford to buy the textbooks and school supplies their children need.

Below:
Haiti requires ten years of primary education, but less than three-quarters of the children under age twelve go to school, and only two-thirds of them will finish primary school.

Left: These older Haitian students attend a vocational college in Port-au-Prince. Other schools for higher education include the University of Haiti. Built in 1944, it is the country's oldest university.

For the children who attend school, most of the course work is in literature and the **humanities**. Rural schools, however, offer **vocational** education and courses in agriculture.

After completing primary school, students must pass exams to go on to secondary school, which lasts three years. Haiti also has several different kinds of schools for higher education.

Religion

Most Haitians are Roman Catholics. White plantation owners began passing on this religion to their slaves in the late 1800s. About 16 percent of Haiti's people belong to Protestant religions. Protestantism became popular in the 1950s, and its followers have increased since then. *Vodun* (voh-DAHN), or voodoo, however, is considered Haiti's national religion. Almost everyone in Haiti, even Catholics and Protestants, practices at least some voodoo.

Left: Because about 80 percent of the people in Haiti are Catholics, Nativity scenes are popular Christmas decorations.

When Haitian slaves were forced to accept their owners' Roman Catholic religion, they began to mix in some of their native voodoo beliefs. Although the Roman Catholic Church is against voodoo, it has put up with some of the ceremonies and practices for many years. The Protestant Church, on the other hand, has made openly practicing any voodoo extremely difficult for its Haitian followers.

Above: These Haitians are taking part in a voodoo ceremony. Voodoo is a religion that comes from West Africa. It involves worshiping the spirits of dead ancestors.

Language

Haiti's two official languages are Haitian Creole and French. Although only about 10 percent of the people speak French, it is considered Haiti's national language because it is the formal language of government and business. Because all Haitians speak Haitian Creole, it is the country's daily language. Also, the government has encouraged the use of Haitian Creole for education and official business. In recent years, more Haitians, especially young people, are speaking English.

Below:
The language on this election poster is Haitian Creole. This language is probably based on French, but it sounds different. It sounds more like some of the African languages spoken by the slaves brought to Haiti.

Literature

Storytelling was Haiti's earliest form of literature. Because so many Haitians could not read or write, they passed on history and folklore verbally from one generation to the next. Storytelling is still popular in Haiti today, with songs often added to the stories.

Much of Haiti's written literature is either about the nation's history or about the difficulties of day-to-day life in Haiti. All Haitian literature had been written in French until, in 1975, author Franck Étienne published the first full-length novel, *Dézafi*, in Haitian Creole.

Arts

The art of Haiti was not widely known until the twentieth century. In 1944, an American artist named DeWitt Peters made Haitian paintings famous in many countries. He also opened the Centre d'Art in Port-au-Prince, which sold Haitian art and made people more aware of Haiti's artistic traditions.

Below: Unlike the lives of the Haitian people, which are often gloomy and difficult, Haitian paintings are very colorful and show great imagination.

Paintings and Handicrafts

The most popular pieces of Haitian art are primitive-style paintings. Haitian farmers had been painting in this style since the 1800s before it was widely recognized. Most primitive artists had no formal training, but with more opportunities for study today, many Haitian artists are combining primitive with other painting styles.

Simple handicrafts, such as oil drum art, Carnival masks, and basketwork, are also important pieces of Haitian art.

Above:
The popularity of Haitian paintings brought attention to the country's handicrafts, too. Haitian crafts include a variety of straw hats.

Music

Lively music is a big part of Haiti's culture. Merengue is one of its most well-known music and dance styles. It started in the 1800s, when Haitian musicians mixed European classical music with African drumming and dancing. *Compas* (KOM-pah) music, which combines merengue, rock 'n' roll, jazz, and voodoo drum rhythms, is very popular among young Haitians.

Above: Prayer flags are another beautiful example of Haitian artistry. Used in voodoo ceremonies, they are pieces of cloth decorated with brightly colored patterns of intricate embroidery and sparkling sequins.

Architecture

A restored **citadel** and the ruins of a palace are two of the famous buildings that attract visitors to Haiti from all over the world. These two pieces of historic architecture were built in the early 1800s by Henri Christophe, who named himself king of Haiti in 1811. The Citadelle LaFerrière and the Palais de Sans Souci are both located near Cap-Haïtien. Other historic buildings in Haiti include the Cathedrale de la Ste. Trinité, in Port-au-Prince.

Below:
The architecture in many Haitian cities features old buildings painted with bright colors. This colorful old building in Port-au-Prince contains offices of the government.

Leisure

Most people in Haiti spend their leisure time with their families. Almost every Saturday evening, families and friends get together to eat, drink, dance, trade jokes, and tell stories. Haitians call this weekly gathering a *bambouche* (bum-BAWSH). A **lottery** called *borlette* (bor-LET) is another popular weekly activity. Haitians also enjoy playing cards and board games.

Below: Although many of Haiti's beautiful beaches are open only to tourists, Haitians still spend a lot of their free time in the sun and the sand at the beaches they are allowed to visit.

Wealthier Haitians have more ways to spend their leisure time. Because they have money, and because they live in the cities, they can go to movies, dance clubs, and theater performances.

Haitians use a lot of their free time for religious activities. These activities help some people forget their problems for a while. Catholics go to Mass even on weekdays. Visits to voodoo temples are also common, but less frequent.

Above: For many Haitians, going to the market is an opportunity to see relatives and friends and to exchange news about families.

Cockfighting

Each Sunday, almost every village and neighborhood in Haiti holds cockfights. A cockfight takes place at a pit called a *gagé* (GAH-zhay). Spectators gather around the pit to watch. Before a fight starts, owners parade their birds around the pit. Each bird has a name. A single cockfight can last as long as half an hour. The fight ends when one of the two birds gets tired.

Below: Watching cockfights is one of the most popular pastimes in Haiti. At these fights, spectators often bet money on the birds they think will win.

Left: Haiti's Michel Gabriel (*left*) battles Chris Armas of the United States for control of the ball during a soccer match in Miami, Florida, in 2000.

Soccer

Haiti's most popular team sport is soccer, but Haitians call the sport football. Professional soccer matches at the Sylvio Cator Stadium in Port-au-Prince attract huge crowds, and, all over the country, Haitians play soccer on dirt roads and in fields.

Holidays and Festivals

Christmas is Haiti's biggest holiday. The celebration starts in mid-December and lasts almost a month. On Christmas Eve, families go to midnight mass and eat a late supper. On Christmas Day, they open gifts and, over several more weeks, share gifts with friends. Haiti's Christmas season includes two other important holidays on January 1 and 2, Independence Day and Ancestor's Day.

Below: A journey to Saut d'Eau is an annual event for many Haitians. The people of Haiti believe that this town's waterfalls can cure illnesses.

Haiti's Carnival festival is a lively celebration of art and culture. It lasts several days during February or March, ending on Ash Wednesday, which is the first day of **Lent**. Musical groups called *ra-ra* (RAH-rah) bands perform often during the forty days of Lent. On Easter Sunday, ra-ra musicians dress in unusual costumes and march from the voodoo temples through the streets of Haiti in colorful processions.

Above: Haiti's Carnival festival includes colorful parades, costumes and masks, and nonstop music and dancing.

Food

Haitian food is a lot like the food of other Caribbean countries, except it is more peppery. It combines flavors from the traditional cooking of Africa, France, Spain, and the United States. Rice is the main ingredient in two of Haiti's most basic dishes, *riz djon-djon* (ree JON-JON), which is rice with small black mushrooms, and *riz pois collés* (ree pwah KUHL-lay), which is rice with red beans.

Left: Millet is a type of grain that grows in Haiti. Haitians often eat crushed millet that has been mixed with water.

Left: Plantains are a common type of fruit in Haiti. They look like green bananas and are eaten roasted, steamed, or fried, often as a dessert.

Because Haiti has many rivers and is practically surrounded by the ocean, dishes made with fish and other types of seafood are common.

Away from the ocean, Haitians like to eat meat, especially pork, goat, and chicken. In rural areas, *griot* (GREE-yoh) is a popular dish of fried pork and *ti-malice* (tee-MAH-liss), which is a very spicy sauce.

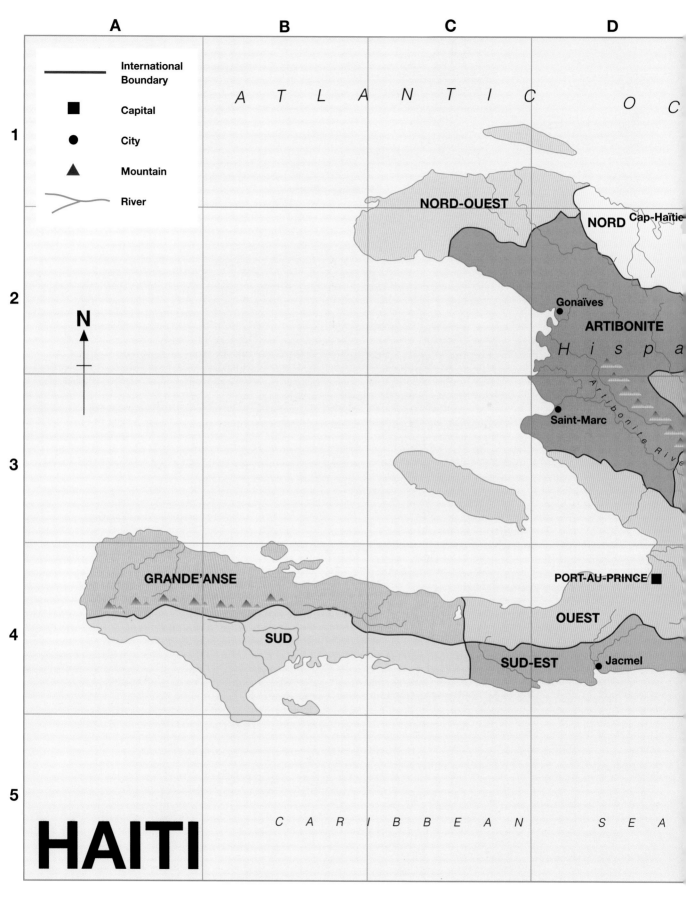

HAITI

42

NORD-EST

CENTRE

aut d'Eau

Étang Saumâtre

▲ *Pic la Selle (8,793 feet/ 2,680 m)*

i o l a

DOMINICAN REPUBLIC

Above: This Haitian painting shows French forces capturing Toussaint L'Ouverture, a leader in the slave uprising of 1791.

Artibonite (department) C2–D3

Artibonite River D2–E3

Atlantic Ocean A1–E1

Cap-Haïtien D2

Caribbean Sea A5–E5

Centre (department) D3–E3

Dominican Republic E1–E5

Étang Saumâtre (lake) E4

Gonaïves D2

Grande'Anse (department) A3–C4

Hispaniola A4–E1

Jacmel D4

Nord (department) D1–E2

Nord-Est (department) E2

Nord-Ouest (department) B2–D1

Ouest (department) C3–E4

Pic la Selle E4

Port-au-Prince D4

Saint-Marc D3

Saut d'Eau E3

Sud (department) A4–C4

Sud-Est (department) C4–E4

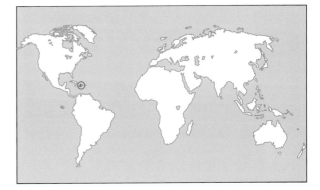

Quick Facts

Official Name	Republic of Haiti
Capital	Port-au-Prince
Official Languages	Haitian Creole and French
Population	7,063,722 (2002 estimate)
Land Area	10,641 square miles (27,560 square km)
Departments	Artibonite, Centre, Grande'Anse, Nord, Nord-Est, Nord-Ouest, Ouest, Sud, Sud-Est
Highest Point	Pic la Selle 8,793 feet (2,680 m)
Major Cities	Cap-Haïtien, Gonaïves, Port-au-Prince
Longest River	Artibonite 174 miles (280 km)
Largest Lake	Étang Saumâtre
Major Holidays	Independence Day (January 1) Carnival (February/March) Easter (March/April) Christmas Day (December 25)
Major Exports	Cocoa, coffee, oils, mangoes
Major Imports	Food, fuels, machinery, transportation equipment, petroleum products
Currency	Gourde (HTG 38.00 = U.S. $1 as of 2003)

Opposite: These Haitian women are selling vegetables on a street in Port-au-Prince.

Glossary

assassinated: killed for political reasons.

citadel: a very large structure protected by strong walls and armed guards or soldiers; a fortress.

civilization: a highly developed society with an established government and culture and a written history.

coat of arms: a specially designed symbol that identifies and represents a particular group, institution, or region.

colonized: settled an area or region of a foreign land under the laws of a distant home government.

commerce: the business of buying, selling, or trading goods.

corrupt: willing to do something wrong or illegal to gain money or power.

deforestation: cutting down or burning trees to clear the land.

democratic: relating to a political system in which people elect representatives to make laws and run the government.

dictator: a ruler who has complete authority over a country.

endangered: in danger of dying out completely, or becoming extinct.

erosion: the process of wind and water slowly wearing away Earth's surface.

ethnic minority: a cultural group that is a small part of a nation's population.

executed: put to death.

humanities: fields of study that are not scientific, such as art or languages.

Lent: the Christian season of fasting during the forty days before Easter.

lottery: a game in which people pay a small amount of money for a chance to win a lot of money or a valuable prize.

mangroves: tropical trees with masses of tangled roots above the ground.

mulattoes: people who have mixed black and white racial ancestry.

navigable: suitable for travel by boat.

peninsulas: long strips of land that are surrounded by water on three sides.

poverty: the state of being without enough money and living necessities, such as food, clothing, and shelter.

republic: a country in which citizens elect their own lawmakers.

scrub: short, woody, bushlike plants.

unstable: not firm, steady, or strong.

vocational: relating to an occupation, profession, or skilled trade.

More Books to Read

Bèl Peyi Mwen. Elizabeth Turnbull (Mountain Maid Self Help Project)

Children Songs from Haiti: Chante Timoun Ayiti. Fequiere Vilsaint (Educa Vision)

Haiti. Countries of the World series. Suzanne Paul Dell'Oro (Capstone Press)

Haiti. Festivals of the World series. Roseline Ngcheong-Lum (Gareth Stevens)

Haiti: Faces and Places. Elma Schemenauer (Child's World)

Painted Dreams. Karen Lynn Williams (Lothrop Lee & Shepard)

Running the Road to ABC. Denize Lauture (Simon & Schuster)

Tap-Tap. Karen Lynn Williams (Clarion Books)

Toussaint L'Ouverture: The Fight for Haiti's Freedom. Walter Dean Myers (Simon & Schuster)

Videos

Caribbean Close-Up: Haiti & The Dominican Republic. Children of the Earth series. (Maryknoll World Productions)

Dominican Republic & Haiti. (Lonely Planet)

Web Sites

pasture.ecn.purdue.edu/~agenhtml/ agenmc/haiti/haiti.html

www.careusa.org/vft/haiti/

www.factmonster.com/ipka/ A0107612.html

Due to the dynamic nature of the Internet, some web sites stay current longer than others. To find additional web sites, use a reliable search engine with one or more of the following keywords to help you locate information about Haiti. Keywords: *Ayiti, Dessalines, François Duvalier, Haitian Creole, Hispaniola, Port-au-Prince, vodun.*

Index